Some white,
some pink.
All lovely,
I think.

Each year when spring returns, robins dance on new grass.

Drowsy bees
sing to swaying
daffodils.

Warm breezes make tulips take a bow.

In Washington, D.C., Japanese cherry trees take center stage. Their tight pink buds open to put on a breathtaking show . . .

around the Tidal Basin . . .

in East Potomac Park . . .

around the Washington Monument . . .

and in
unexpected
pockets here
and there.

From a distance, craggy branches
are lost in billowing clouds of snowy
white and soft shades of pink.

Up close, flower
clusters bigger
than your fist cling
to gnarled twigs.

Branches sweep low,
bringing sweet blossoms
close enough to sniff.

Some trees have been showing off since 1912, when the people of Tokyo, Japan, sent them as a gift of friendship to America.

New trees are planted now and then, but one thing never changes . . .

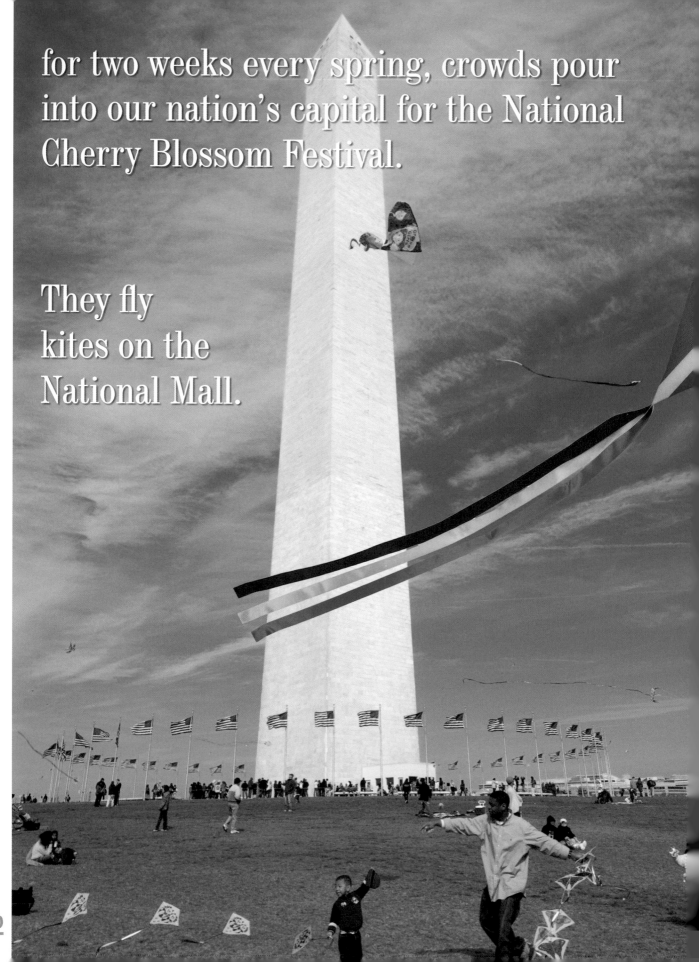

for two weeks every spring, crowds pour into our nation's capital for the National Cherry Blossom Festival.

They fly kites on the National Mall.

They watch
a parade and
cheer for
the Cherry
Blossom
Queen.

They enjoy carnival
rides, paddleboats,
a bike rally . . .

and take pictures.

LOTS of pictures!

Too soon, the party's over.
Delicate petals fade, then fall.

In their place
dark leaves
and small
bright cherries
appear.

Stroll among the trees in summer, fall, or winter, and it's easy to forget the magic hiding inside.

But spring remembers . . .

and can hardly wait to put on another show.